J
M
Y
A

Kid Pick!

Title: _____

Author: _____

Picked by: _____

_____

Why I love this book:

_____

_____

Author:
Fiona Macdonald studied history at
Cambridge University and at the University of
East Anglia. She has taught in schools, adult
education, and college and is the author of
numerous books for children on historical topics.

Artist:
David Antram was born in Brighton in 1958.
He studied at Eastbourne College of Art and then
worked in advertising for fifteen years before
becoming a full-time artist. He has illustrated
many children's nonfiction books.

Series Creator:
David Salariya was born in Dundee, Scotland.
He has illustrated a wide range of books and has
created and designed many new series for
publishers both in the UK and overseas. In 1989
he established The Salariya Book Company. He
lives in Brighton with his wife, illustrator Shirley
Willis, and their son Jonathan.

Editor:
Karen Barker Smith

Assistant Editor:
Stephanie Cole

© The Salariya Book Company Ltd MMI

Created, designed, and produced by
The Salariya Book Company Ltd
25 Marlborough Place, Brighton BN1 1UB

ISBN 0-531-14602-2 (Lib. Bdg.)
ISBN 0-531-16209-5 (Pbk.)

Published in the United States by Franklin Watts
A Division of Scholastic Inc.
90 Sherman Turnpike, Danbury, CT 06816

A CIP catalog record for this title is
available from the Library of Congress.

Repro by Modern Age.

Printed in China.

You Wouldn't Want to Be an Aztec Sacrifice!

Do you have the heart for it?

Written by
Fiona Macdonald

Illustrated by
David Antram

Created and designed by
David Salariya

Gruesome Things You'd Rather Not Know

W
FRANKLIN WATTS
A Division of Scholastic Inc.

NEW YORK • TORONTO • LONDON • AUCKLAND • SYDNEY
MEXICO CITY • NEW DELHI • HONG KONG
DANBURY, CONNECTICUT

Contents

Introduction

I t is the late fifteenth century in Mesoamerica, the area where North and South America meet. You live in a prosperous Mexican city that was conquered by the Aztecs in 1428.

The Aztecs are an energetic and warlike people who are now at the height of their power. They arrived in Mexico around 1200. At first they lived peacefully among your people, working as soldiers and servants. They soon made their presence felt more strongly when they fought and won a war against their masters. In 1325, the Aztecs settled on an island in the middle of a swampy lake and built a vast new city called Tenochtitlan.

Since then, the Aztecs have set out to take over all the neighboring lands. They often demand goods from the cities they have conquered. You have also heard that they take captives and kill them as offerings to their gods. The Aztecs can be ruthless when they are seeking captives. One thing you know for sure is that you wouldn't want to be an Aztec sacrifice!

Great Expectations

ou are a young man from a noble family in the Central Valley of Mexico. You have a comfortable home, plenty of food, and a happy family. You enjoy strength and good health.

If it weren't for your overlords, the Aztecs, you would be content with your life. The Aztecs are fearsome warriors, and everybody is scared of them. Your servants have heard a rumor that Aztec ambassadors will soon be arriving in your city. They visit conquered peoples every year, and you dread their arrival.

Mesoamerica

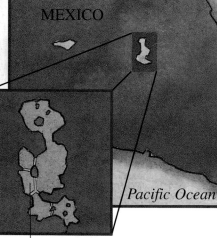

MEXICO

Gulf of Mexico

Pacific Ocean

Tenochtitlan

The Aztecs live in Mesoamerica, where North and South America meet. Their capital city, Tenochtitlan, is built on an island in a lake in the Central Valley of Mexico.

What You Like About Your Life:

YOU GOT MARRIED at age twenty to a girl chosen by your parents. Now you have an adorable baby son.

YOU WERE WELL FED and cared for in childhood, and you grew up healthy. You exercise to keep in shape.

YOU LIVE with you wife and child in you parents' house. It is very large and has a spacious courtyard.

6

They'll be here any day now!

Handy Hint

Make offerings to your city's guardian god — he might protect you from the Aztecs!

YOU EAT plenty of healthy food, mostly maize and fresh vegetables. You also eat lots of spicy foods.

YOU OWN fine clothes, including a feathered headdress and gold jewelry.

YOU WERE SENT TO SCHOOL as a boy and are able to read, write, and do simple calculations.

YOU ARE RESPECTED by the other citizens because of your nobility.

Hand It Over! Tribute Payments

Picture-Writing

Aztec scribes use picture-writing to draw up lists of all the goods taken as tribute. The most valuable tribute goods include cloaks, blankets, feathers, and cotton.

Finger (a) = 1

Knife (b) = 20

Feather (c) = 400

Shield (d) = 800

It's true! Aztec ambassadors, accompanied by well-armed bodyguards, have just arrived in your city. They come every year to demand goods, known as tribute, which they take back to their capital city. Handing over so much tribute is a great burden for your city — but worse is to come. The Aztecs challenge you to a "flowery war." They want to fight you so they can take some of you captive in battle.

a

b

c

d

400 fine cloaks

20 warrior outfits

440 boxes of cotton

40 shields

22 boxes of beans

400 baskets of chili peppers

What more do you want? Blood?

FLOWERY WARS are not battles where soldiers throw plants at one another. They are ritual wars fought by the Aztecs to win captives for sacrifice.

Thwack!

Handy Hint

Don't try to cheat as you hand over tribute payments. Aztec spies have sharp eyes and keep a careful record of everything.

Get Ready – The Aztecs Are Coming!

Choose Your Weapon:

Bow and arrows

Spear

Battleaxe

Club with obsidian blades

It's time to defend your city — the Aztecs are on the warpath! For days they have been preparing for the flowery war. The great square in the center of their capital city, Tenochtitlan, has resounded to the beat of a huge war drum. Priests have been chanting and dancing on the temple steps, and hundreds of well-trained soldiers have been getting their weapons and armor ready. Led by its famous noble warriors, the Aztec army has marched out of the city and is now making its way toward you! All you can do is prepare your own weapons and wait for the Aztecs to arrive.

You Will Need:

A BOW AND ARROWS, plus a spear, to attack distant enemies, and a sharp battleaxe or warclub for hand-to-hand fighting.

Magic shield

A MAGIC SHIELD decorated with magic patterns. Many soldiers believe the magic will protect them on the battlefield.

PADDED ARMOR. Soak your thickly padded suit in salt water. This will make it even stronger.

Disaster! Captured in Battle

It's all over! You fought bravely, but you had particularly bad luck — during the battle, you came face to face with a fearsome Eagle Knight. He seemed anxious not to harm you. Instead, he dragged you from the battlefield to join a large group of captives. Now that the battle is over, the terrible truth is beginning to sink in. You might never see your home and family again.

Jaguar Knight

Eagle Knight

Gotcha!

TOP AZTEC WARRIORS belong to one of two elite brotherhoods — the Jaguar or the Eagle Knights. They wear costumes made from jaguar skin or eagle feathers, which they believe give them the strength of wild beasts.

NOVICE SOLDIERS always have long hair. Be on your guard if you meet one — he'll be eager to get you! Young Aztec warriors are not allowed to cut their hair and arrange it in a top-knot style until they have proved their manhood by killing an enemy or taking captives.

IF YOU ARE INJURED, try traditional remedies. Bathing wounds in salt water kills germs. Raw chili peppers, crushed and rubbed on the skin, help numb pain. Herbal mixtures also act as anesthetics. You can sew wounds up using cactus spines as needles.

Chili peppers

Salt bath

Herbal mixture

Cactus needle

Handy Hint

If you want to make friends with an Aztec warrior, give him flowers. Off-duty warriors like to stroll through the streets, dressed in their best and carrying flowers and herbs.

Take this!

Crack!!!

13

A Long Desert Walk

IN THE DESERT, even the plants are unfriendly! You'll find no place to hide behind prickly cacti, spindly sage bushes, or tall, thin stalks of maize.

Cacti

Sage

Maize

With your hands tied behind your back, you have been roped together with many other captives, mostly strong young warriors like yourself. You are hungry, thirsty, and exhausted. The desert dust chokes you, and the hot sun half blinds you as you stumble along a narrow mountain track. You are all being taken to Tenochtitlan, which you can see in the distance. You have heard that it is a magnificent city, full of fine buildings and surrounded by fertile gardens. But any admiring thoughts are far from your mind. You just want to escape!

Even If You Escape...

YOU might die of thirst...

or be driven mad by the loneliness...

or be eaten by wild animals...

or freeze to death overnight...

or even meet an angry Aztec god!

14

Handpicked! Who Will Be Chosen?

Are You Top Quality?

IF YOU ARE unhealthy, scarred, diseased, ugly, or fat, the Aztecs will not choose you for sacrifice. Instead you will be forced to work as a slave.

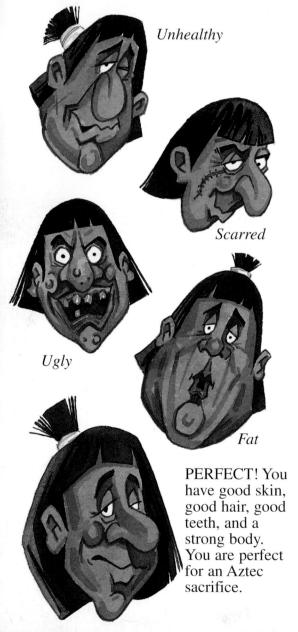

Unhealthy

Scarred

Ugly

Fat

PERFECT! You have good skin, good hair, good teeth, and a strong body. You are perfect for an Aztec sacrifice.

When you reach the Aztec capital city, you are taken to a prison and crammed inside a wooden cage along with other captives. Guards bring you food and water every day. One morning, you are visited by some of the priests from the Aztecs' most important temple. They spend a long time looking at you through the bars of your cage, and the scribes who accompany them write notes on pieces of fig-bark paper. It's a good thing you can't read Aztec picture-writing — otherwise you would learn that your name is being added to the list of prisoners chosen for sacrifice!

AZTEC PRIESTS are sent to temple schools when young and taught to read, write, and calculate (a). They also learn astronomy and religion (b). They endure long nights alone on mountainsides (c) to make them physically and mentally tough. They also help with temple rituals (d).

a

b

c

d

A Gift Fit for the Gods

THE AZTECS BELIEVE that the gods will be angry and might destroy the world if they don't offer them sacrifices. Aztec scribes say that this has already happened four times. Previous worlds were destroyed by a hungry tiger, wind, rain, and a flood. Each time the world was reborn. Next time, however, the world will end once and for all in a massive earthquake.

h, no! The guards tell you that the priests have chosen you to be sacrificed as a gift to their gods. You are horrified by this news, but you also understand. Many cultures in Mesoamerica offer human sacrifices to the gods. The gods provide rain, sunshine, and everything else to keep humanity alive, so you must offer them gifts in return. Now, as you sit in your prison cage, only one thought fills your mind. To which god will you be sacrificed?

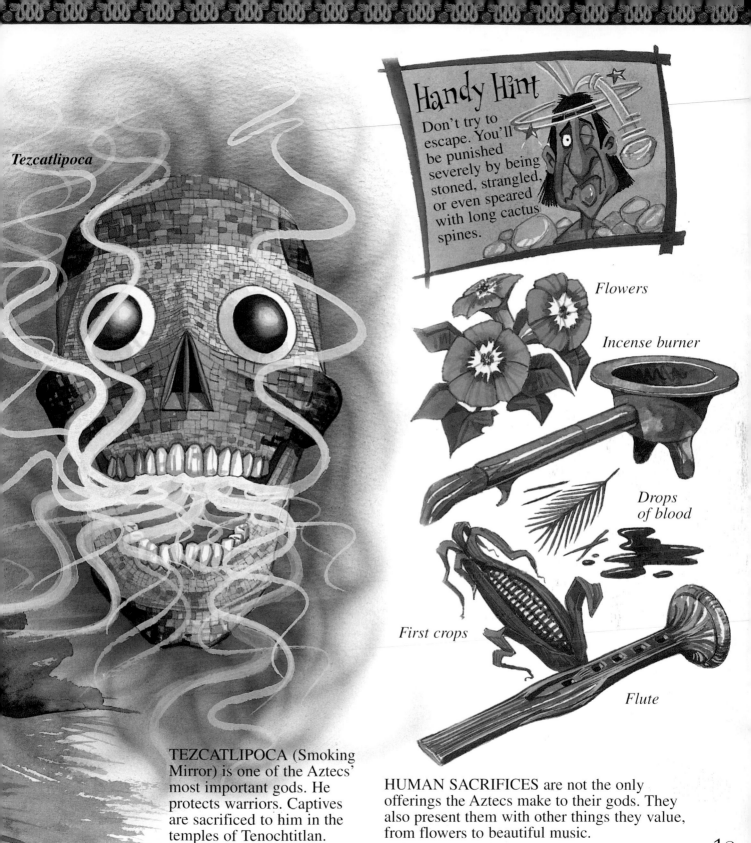

Tezcatlipoca

Handy Hint

Don't try to escape. You'll be punished severely by being stoned, strangled, or even speared with long cactus spines.

Flowers

Incense burner

Drops of blood

First crops

Flute

TEZCATLIPOCA (Smoking Mirror) is one of the Aztecs' most important gods. He protects warriors. Captives are sacrificed to him in the temples of Tenochtitlan.

HUMAN SACRIFICES are not the only offerings the Aztecs make to their gods. They also present them with other things they value, from flowers to beautiful music.

19

A Special Day

Soon you learn that the Aztecs are planning a great festival called the New Fire Ceremony. One of their most important festivals, it only happens once every fifty-two years. All lights and fires are put out for five days, and everyone fears the world will end.

AZTEC PRIESTS AND SCRIBES make careful observations of the sun, moon, stars, and planets. They measure time using a calendar that has 260 days. Each year is divided into 13 months, each with 20 days.

Aztec farmers use a different calendar, based on the movements of the sun. It has 360 days, plus 5 extra, unlucky ones. After 73 priests' years and 52 farmers' years, the two calendar cycles end on the same day. This is when the New Fire Ceremony is held.

Priests' calendar

Farmers' calendar

At the end of the five days, priests look for Venus, the evening star, in the sky. When it appears, they sacrifice a captive and light the New Fire on him. Then the Aztecs rejoice.

Handy Hint

Hope to be chosen to play in the ball game. If you win, you'll have a chance of surviving, because only the losing team is sacrificed!

Don't let it go out!

TO CALCULATE days for festivals and sacrifices, Aztec priests and scribes use yet another calendar based on the planet Venus (the evening star). Each Venus year is 584 days long.

THE BALL GAME is a religious ritual as well as a sport. Players keep a rubber ball moving in the court to give energy to the sun.

21

How Will You Meet Your End?

Most captives are sacrificed by having their hearts cut out with a sharp knife. This is performed so quickly that it is almost painless. Some captives are beheaded, which is also a quick and merciful way to be sacrificed. However, there are also much slower and nastier ways of being killed. You could be thrown into a lake and left to drown, or you could be skinned alive. If you are a warrior, you could be tied to a stone and forced to fight a senior Aztec warrior using weapons made from feathers and wood.

You Might Be:

FLAYED (skinned). In the springtime, captives are sacrificed to Xipe Totec, the god of new young plants. The captives' skins are cut off and used to dress the god's statue.

BEHEADED. Just before harvest, a person the same height as the standing maize is killed by having his head chopped off.

DROWNED. Young people are thrown into lakes as offerings to Tlaloc, the god of water and life-giving rain.

Ha! You'll have to try harder than that!

22

SACRIFICIAL KNIVES are made from flint, obsidian, or semiprecious stone. They are often beautifully decorated with images of the gods. The Aztecs do not know how to make knives from iron or steel, but they are expert stone-workers. These knives are very sharp!

Flint knife

Obsidian knife

W h ó ó s h !

Up the Temple Steps....

Sounds of drumming and chanting echo around the city as the festival approaches. At dawn, the guards make you drink a strange-tasting potion, which makes you feel drowsy. Along with thousands of other captives, you walk to the temple at the center of Tenochtitlan. You see priests with their bodies painted black and red and with wild, matted hair. Behind them, you glimpse fearsome statues of the gods. Walking slowly up the temple steps, you are grabbed by five priests and flung on your back across a sacrificial stone. You see no more...

YOU MIGHT FEEL LOST in the crowds of people. On some occasions, the Aztecs kill huge numbers of captives. It is said that 20,000 men were sacrificed when the Great Temple in the center of Tenochtitlan was dedicated in 1487.

You Are Probably Not Too Scared Because...

AN HERBAL POTION makes you feel drowsy and peaceful.

DRUMMING and chanting lull you into a trance-like state.

AFTER WEEKS in prison, you have forgotten what life was like before.

THE PRIESTS are so awe-inspiring that you feel you have to obey them.

What Happens to Your Body?

Honored Offerings:

YOUR HEART, the most precious part of the sacrifice, will be held in a *chac-mool* carved from stone.

YOUR HEAD will be kept in a skull rack outside the temple.

YOUR BLOOD will be poured down the temple steps.

YOUR ARMS AND LEGS will be eaten as a religious feast.

You die quickly and with little pain, but the sacrifice is not over yet. The priests cut your heart from your body and raise it high toward the sky to show it to the gods. Then they place it in a special container, called a *chac-mool*, as an offering to the gods. Next, they cut off your head and display it in a skull rack along with hundreds of others. This gives the temple extra "spirit-power." Finally, your blood is poured down the temple steps, and your limbs are tossed to the crowds of worshipers below. The warrior who captured you collects the limbs and takes them home. He cooks and eats your sacrificed flesh. This is a way of sharing a holy meal and linking heaven and Earth.

THE AZTECS genuinely believe that the sun will only continue to shine if sacrifices are offered to it. They do not view the ritual of sacrifice as cruel or bloodthirsty, because it ensures that life will continue.

Will Your Spirit Become a Butterfly?

Like many other Mesoamerican people, you have always believed that your spirit would live on after death, whatever happened to your body. Because you fought bravely while you were alive and died bravely, too, your spirit will become a beautiful butterfly. It will spend some time on earth, bringing joy to the people who see it. Then, finally, it will fly up to heaven to make its home with the sun. Other people are not so lucky. The Aztecs believe that some unhappy spirits have to make a long, miserable journey through the underworld before they finally perish in hell. Some ghosts are condemned to haunt the Earth forever, bringing fear to all who see them.

SOME SPIRITS, like the ghosts of executed criminals, are said to haunt the streets at night.

Heavens above – thank the gods that's over!

Handy Hint

Feel proud, strong, and free! Every time the Aztecs see a butterfly on Earth, they think of people like you.

THE SPIRITS of women who have died in childbirth are said to terrify travelers at crossroads.

Glossary

Ambassadors
Important officials who are sent abroad to represent their country.

Anesthetic
A drug that makes people sleepy and unable to feel pain.

Astronomy
The study of the sun, moon, stars, and planets.

Aztecs
A Mesoamerican people who lived in central and northern Mexico. They were most powerful between around 1350 and 1520.

Chac-mool
A stone statue in the shape of a dying warrior or water god carrying a dish in his arms. The dish was used to hold blood or hearts from human sacrifices.

Dedicated
Given to, or named for, a god.

Fig bark
The bark of tropical fig trees. It was carefully removed, smoothed, and flattened to make Aztec folding books.

Flint
A hard stone formed in chalky soils. It can be carefully chipped, using stone hammers, to create axes, knives, and other sharp tools.

Flowery wars
Wars fought between the Aztecs and other peoples in Mexico. By fighting, the Aztecs hoped to win captives to sacrifice to their gods.

Guardian god
A god who protects a people or a place.

Incense
A sweet-smelling substance often burned in holy places such as temples.

Novice
A beginner or trainee.

Obsidian
A black, glassy stone produced when volcanoes erupt.

Overlords
People who rule over or control other peoples.

Mesoamerica
The region where North and South America meet. Today, Mesoamerica includes the countries of Mexico, Guatemala, Honduras, El Salvador, and Belize.

Picture-writing
A way of writing using pictures instead of letters.

Potion
A drink of medicine, poison, or supposedly magic liquid.

Ritual
A ceremony that is repeated at special times, such as during religious festivals.

Sacrifice
A person or animal that is killed as an offering, usually to the gods.

Scribe
Person trained in the skills of reading and writing Aztec picture-symbols.

Skull rack
A wood or stone rack, designed to contain hundreds of human skulls, that stood outside Aztec temples.

Tribute
Taxes paid in goods by conquered people to their conquerors.

Venus
One of the planets of the solar system. Like the Earth, it orbits the sun.

Xipe Totec
The Aztec god of fertility. He protected shoots of corn plants.

Index

PICTURE LIBRARY

DRAGONS
AND LIZARDS

PICTURE LIBRARY
DRAGONS AND LIZARDS

Norman Barrett

Franklin Watts

New York   London   Sydney   Toronto

© 1991 Franklin Watts

Franklin Watts, Inc
387 Park Avenue South
New York, NY 10016

Printed in the United Kingdom

Designed by
Barrett and Weintroub

Research by
Deborah Spring

Picture Research by
Ruth Sonntag

Photographs by
Survival Anglia
Australian Overseas Information
    Service, London
Australian Tourist Commission
Norman Barrett
Michael Chinery
Northern Territory Tourist Commission
Queensland Tourist and Travel
    Corporation
Government of Western Australia

Illustration by
Rhoda and Robert Burns

Technical Consultant
Michael Chinery

Library of Congress Cataloging-in-Publication Data

Barrett, Norman S.
    Dragons and lizards/Norman Barrett : [photographs by Survival
Anglia ... et al. : illustrations by Rhoda and Robert Burns.]
        p. cm. — (Picture library)
    Includes index.
    Summary: A look at the feeding habits, reproductive behavior, and
other life functions of lizards living in desert, tropical, and
temperate environments.
    ISBN 0-531-14111-X
    1. Lizards — Juvenile literature. [1. Lizards.] I. Burns.
Rhoda, Ill. II. Burns, Robert, Ill. III. Survival Anglia Ltd.
IV. Title.   V. Series.
QL666.L2B19 1991
597.95—dc20   90-43335
                                                        CIP
                                                         AC

Contents

Introduction

Lizards are reptiles closely related to snakes. Like snakes, they are covered with horny scales. There are nearly 4,000 different species (kinds) of lizards, and they live in most parts of the world.

Lizards live in all kinds of habitats, from deserts to forests to seashores. Many are good swimmers.

Lizards range in size from a few centimeters to as much as 3 meters (10 ft) long.

△ The perentie is a monitor lizard that lives in the deserts of Australia. Perenties grow to as much as 2.5 m (8 ft) long. Monitors have heavy, scaly folds of loose skin. They have five clawed toes on each limb.

Many kinds of lizards are called dragons. They have a rough, spiny skin, sharp claws and large eyes. They live mostly in hot, dry areas.

Some lizards have no legs, or very short weak ones. These include the various kinds of skinks.

Geckos are lizards that have claws which they can draw in, like those of a cat. They have suction pads on their feet, too, so they can climb smooth surfaces. They can even run upside down across ceilings.

△ A bearded dragon displaying its "beard," a loose collar of skin around its neck. It does this in order to appear fierce when disturbed by an enemy, or to threaten a rival male.

Looking at dragons and lizards

Eye has moveable eyelid in most lizards. Many lizards have very good eyesight for locating prey

Ear opening

Tough skin with rows of overlapping scales gives protection against predators and stops the body from drying out in the heat

Hind legs are usually longer and more powerful than front legs. Some lizards run only on their hind legs

Legs – most lizards have four well developed legs. But there are several families of legless lizards

Suction pads enable a gecko to climb up the smoothest surfaces

Tail used for balancing when running or climbing. May also be lashed at enemies. Can be used to store body fat

Climbing

Geckos are excellent climbers and can move easily up vertical walls and even upside down across ceilings. Some kinds of geckos have suction pads on their feet, while others have sharp claws to hook into wood or plaster as they climb.

Other geckos have thin toes tipped with claws

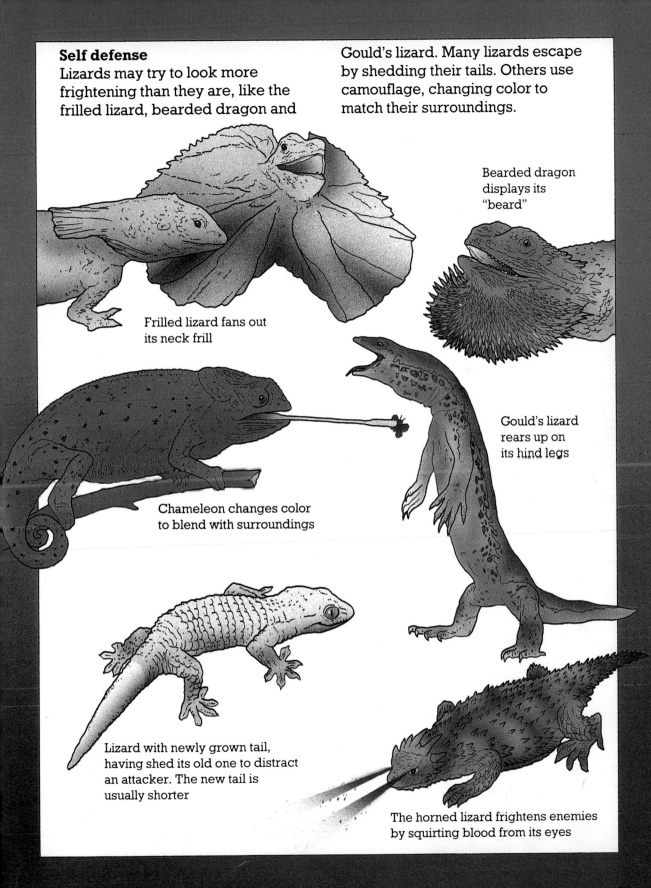

Self defense

Lizards may try to look more frightening than they are, like the frilled lizard, bearded dragon and Gould's lizard. Many lizards escape by shedding their tails. Others use camouflage, changing color to match their surroundings.

Bearded dragon displays its "beard"

Frilled lizard fans out its neck frill

Gould's lizard rears up on its hind legs

Chameleon changes color to blend with surroundings

Lizard with newly grown tail, having shed its old one to distract an attacker. The new tail is usually shorter

The horned lizard frightens enemies by squirting blood from its eyes

Life of lizards

Lizards are cold-blooded animals. Unlike mammals and birds, they do not have a built in temperature control. They need warmth, and most are active only in sunshine. In hot, dry habitats, their waterproof skin prevents the loss of body moisture.

Lizards eat a wide variety of food, depending on where they live. Many species eat insects and other small animals, including smaller lizards. A few lizards eat plants.

△ Lizards, like other reptiles, need to take in heat at the beginning of the day. The sungazer, pictured here, is so-called because of its habit of staring into the sun in the early morning.

▷ A chameleon eating a grasshopper. Most lizards seize their prey in their mouths and swallow it. Chameleons have long, sticky tongues which they shoot out at high speed to capture insects.

Many lizards avoid their enemies by camouflage – blending in with their surroundings. Tree lizards are the color of bark or leaves and lizards that live in the desert blend in with the color of the sand or rock.

Chameleons and some other lizards have the ability to change their color and skin pattern. Chemicals in their body react to light or temperature changes or to fright, and affect the skin coloring.

◁ The Australian frilled lizard spends most of its time camouflaged in the trees hunting for insects. On the ground it is more visible to its enemies. When threatened, it opens its mouth with a hiss and fans out the frill around its neck.

Most European lizards belong to a group called lacertids, which have long, slender tails. They feed mainly on insects and other small creatures. Most of them hibernate (sleep) through the winter.

△ A European green lizard warming its body on a sunny rock.

▷ One of the 15 species of wall lizards found in Europe.

The marine iguana is an unusual lizard that lives on the tropical Galapagos Islands. It is the only sea lizard and plunges into the cold ocean surrounding the islands in order to feed on seaweed. This would drastically lower the body temperature of other lizards. But marine iguanas can keep their blood near the center of their body, so that it does not cool down too much before they come out into the sun again.

△ A colony of marine iguanas bask in the sun on the Galapagos Islands.

Most species of lizards lay eggs, although a few give birth to live young. Eggs are usually laid in a moist place, and the baby lizards left to hatch and to fend for themselves. But some lizards protect their eggs until the young are hatched.

▷ The Texas alligator lizard protects her eggs.

▽ A baby gecko hatching out of its egg.

Giant lizards

The worlds largest lizards belong to two separate families, the monitors and the iguanas. The giants of these families have few enemies.

Monitors live in southern Asia, Africa and Australia and nearby islands. They have a long head and neck and are fierce predators.

Iguanas are found mainly in the Americas, where most of them live in wooded areas and often climb trees. They feed mainly on plants.

△ Land iguanas of the Galapagos, a group of islands in the Pacific Ocean near South America. They eat cacti, insects, and other flowers and plants.

▷ The lace monitor, which can grow to 2 m (6½ ft), is common in eastern Australia.

▽ An Asian water monitor drinking. A feature of monitor lizards is their long forked tongue, which can be clearly seen in the picture. Like snakes, lizards constantly flick out their tongues to explore their surroundings.

△ A savannah monitor
killing a snake in Africa.
Monitors will eat almost
anything they can kill.

◁ A marine iguana.

▷ Common, or green,
iguanas live in South
and Central America
and on some Caribbean
islands. They have a
crest of scales running
along their back and
tail, and a flap of skin
called a "dewlap" at
their throat.

Tree lizards

Lizards from many different families live in forests. These include some of the giant lizards, such as the lace monitor and the green iguana. Other tree lizards include geckos, agamids, anoles and chameleons.

Lizards that live in trees are well equipped for climbing. Their coloring usually blends with their surroundings so that they can hide from both their enemies and their own prey.

△ The green anole, a native of Florida. There are more than 150 species of anoles, small members of the iguana family. Like chameleons, they can change their color. But unlike the short and fat chameleons, anoles are streamlined, with long tails and legs and a narrow head.

▷ Boyd's forest dragon of Australia, an agamid, is one of the larger tree-dwelling lizards.

◁ The chameleon is one of the few lizards that have grasping, or "prehensile," tails. When not in use, the tail is usually coiled up like a spring.

▽ Geckos are active mainly at night and have large eyes.

△ Many geckos have long tails which they use for balance when climbing. This green gecko from New Zealand can also use its tail for grasping, like a chameleon.

▷ Leseur's water dragon is an agamid from eastern Australia. It grows to about 70 cm (28 in) and is found in trees along rivers or coasts.

23

Desert lizards

A variety of lizards are found in deserts, including species of monitors, iguanas and geckos.

As a group, lizards are the most successful animals to adapt to dry desert conditions. They can stand more heat than mammals or birds and need less food.

Some lizards have specially adapted feet for moving across the sand. Others avoid predators or the heat of the sun by "swimming" through the sand.

△ A fringe-toed lizard emerges from the sand of the Mojave Desert, in California. Its toes are fringed with scales which help it to run across the loose surface at great speed before diving into the sand. It can "swim" through the sand as a defense against predators or to keep out of the sun.

▷ The collared lizard is an agile creature that lives in the rocky deserts of Mexico and the United States.

△ The moloch, or thorny devil, of the sandy Australian deserts is covered with sharp, spiny scales. These are more than just for protection. At night, moisture condenses on them from the air and is drawn down fine grooves into its mouth.

◁ The web footed gecko lives among the sand dunes of Africa's Namib Desert.

Legless lizards and skinks

Legless lizards are found in many parts of the world and include the European slow worm and glass lizard. Most live on the ground, and look and move like snakes, but they have eyelids, which are absent in snakes.

Skinks represent the largest family of lizards, with over 1,000 species. Most of them have short legs or no legs at all. They live on the ground in all kinds of habitats.

◁ Most skinks have short legs and long, tapering tails.

▽ A snake lizard slithers across the ground.

The story of lizards

△ A land iguana gazes out over a volcanic crater on the Galapagos Islands, looking like a prehistoric monster on a prehistoric landscape. Lizards are survivors from the Age of Reptiles, when dinosaurs ruled the world.

Reptiles that survived

Lizards are descendants of reptiles that lived when dinosaurs ruled the world, hundreds of millions of years ago. The word "dinosaur" means terrible lizard, but dinosaurs are not the ancestors of lizards. When the dinosaurs died out, other reptiles survived. These included the lizards.

Descended from amphibians

It is thought that reptiles evolved (developed over millions of years) from amphibians. Amphibians are animals, such as frogs and newts, that live part of their life in water and part on land. Reptiles were able to move away from water because they developed eggs that could be laid on land. These have thick shells and membranes that prevent the loss of moisture. This enabled reptiles to leave the swamps and lakes inhabited by amphibians, and spread to all kinds of habitats. The most successful reptiles have been the lizards and the snakes which evolved from them.

Convergent evolution

As lizards spread to different parts of the world, they adapted to new habitats, such as rainforests and sandy deserts. The evolution and extinction of a species depends on many things, such as climate, available food and competition from other species – in other words, the habitat. Similar habitats will often result in the evolution of similar species. This is called convergent evolution.

Two lizards provide a good example of this, the horned lizard of the deserts of the American Southwest and the thorny devil of the Australian deserts. These lizards have developed separately, from different ancestors, into similar animals with similar ways of life, including their special diet of ants.

Survival

The greatest enemy of the lizard is the human race. As with other animals, many species of lizard are in danger of extinction because of loss of habitat. Forests are cut down, wild country is turned into farmland, industry spreads pollution, and so on.

In some countries, iguanas and other lizards are hunted for food, and lizard skin is used to make products such as handbags.

Many lizards, particularly the endangered species, are now protected by law.

△ A horned lizard from the Mojave Desert in California.

△ A thorny devil from the Australian desert.

Facts and records

△ Komodo dragons feeding.

Largest lizard
The largest lizard in the world is the Komodo dragon, a monitor often reaching 3 m (10 ft) in length and weighing 135 kg (300 lb). It is found on Komodo and some other Indonesian islands. Its prey includes large mammals such as deer and pigs. It is now strictly protected by the Indonesian government, and cannot even be exported to zoos.

△ A Gila monster in the Sonora Desert, in Mexico. It stores fat in its chunky tail and uses this up when food is hard to find.

Poisonous lizards
There are only two species of venomous lizards, the Gila monster and the Mexican beaded lizard. They live in the deserts of the southwestern United States and Central America. Unlike snakes, they do not inject venom into their prey – small mammals and birds. The poison flows into the wound through grooves in their teeth as they chew their prey.

△ A goanna, a giant monitor lizard from Australia.

Goannas
When early European settlers first saw the giant lizards of Australia, they thought they were iguanas, so that is what they called them. This gradually became "goannas," and these great monitor lizards are still called goannas in Australia.

Glossary

Agamids
A family of about 300 species of lizards that live mainly in Africa, Asia and Australia and are similar to the iguanas.

Anoles
A large group of small lizards belonging to the iguana family.

Chameleons
A family of about 100 species of lizards, best known for their ability to change color and for their long tongues.

Cold-blooded
Lizards and other animals whose body temperature is determined by the temperature of their surroundings are called cold-blooded animals.

Dinosaurs
A group of many kinds of reptiles, some of them huge, that lived millions of years ago.

Dragon
A common name given to some kinds of lizards.

Evolution
The development of species, usually over millions of years.

Extinction
The dying out of a species.

Geckos
A family of more than 800 species of small lizards found mainly in the tropics and subtropics.

Habitat
The surroundings in which a particular species lives, including climate, character of the land or water, and plant and other animal life present.

Iguanas
A family of about 650 species of large and small lizards that live mainly in the Americas.

Monitors
A family of about 30 species found mainly in Australia, Africa and Southeast Asia, and including most of the world's largest lizards.

Predators
Animals that eat other creatures.

Skinks
A large family of small lizards with 1,000 or more species, most of which have small, weak legs.

Index